CROSS STITCH
Special Bibs
for SPECIAL BABIES

ALL BABIES ARE SPECIAL. Choose from 14 simple designs and two different alphabets to personalize a bib for your baby. Designs vary from lively fruit and veggies to cute bunnies and bears.

LEISURE ARTS, INC.
LITTLE ROCK, AR

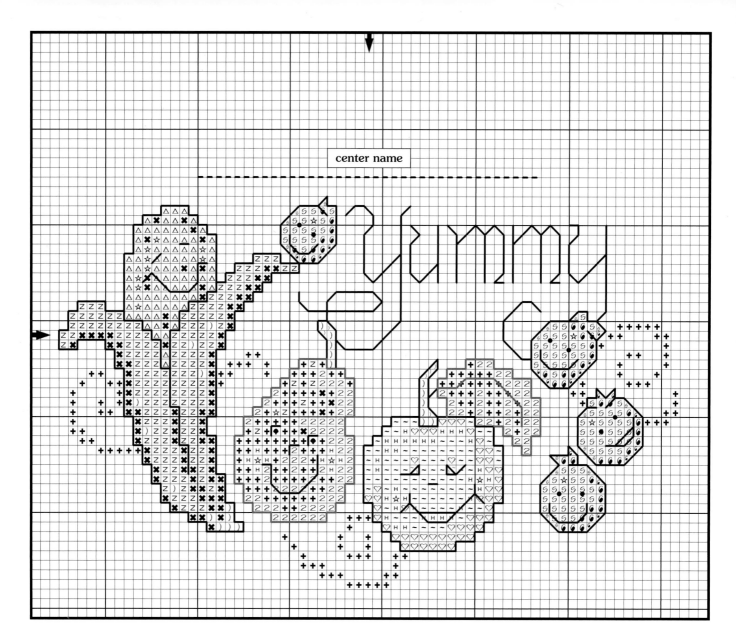

FRUIT

X	DMC	¼X	B'ST	ANC.	COLOR
☆	blanc			2	white
	312		╱*	979	blue
~	350	╱		11	coral
H	352			9	lt coral
△	677			886	lt gold
Z	726			295	yellow
5	794	╱		175	lt royal blue
♡	817			13	dk coral
)	838	╱	╱*	1088	brown
	895		╱	1044	hunter green
2	3347			266	yellow green
+	3348			264	lt yellow green
6	3807	╱		122	royal blue
✖	3852			306	gold
●*	312			979	blue Fr. Knot
●*	838			1088	brown Fr. Knot

*DMC 312 for wording, blueberries and French Knots in blueberries. DMC 838 for all other backstitch and French Knots.

Note: Personalize design with DMC 794 using alphabet on pg. 19.

Design was stitched on a Charles Craft White "Baby Soft" Infant Bib (Item #BB-3650-6750) with a 14 count insert (design size 4⁷⁄₈" x 3⁷⁄₈"). Three strands of floss were used for Cross Stitch and 1 strand for Backstitch and French Knots.

Stitch Count (67w x 53h)
14 count   4⁷⁄₈"   x   3⁷⁄₈"
16 count   4¹⁄₄"   x   3³⁄₈"
18 count   3³⁄₄"   x   3"

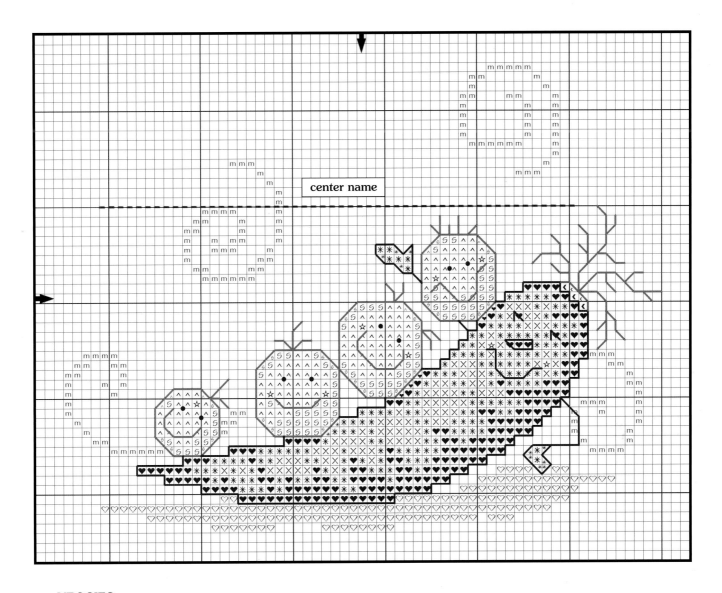

center name

VEGGIES

X DMC	1/4X	B'ST	ANC.	COLOR
☆ blanc			2	white
m 727			293	lt yellow
✳ 740	⟋✳		316	lt orange
✕ 742			303	yellow
838		⟋	1088	brown
❮ 910	⟋❮	⟋	229	dk green
♥ 947	⟋♥		330	orange
⑤ 954	⟋⑤		203	green
∧ 955	⟋∧		206	lt green
♡ 3325			129	blue
● 910			229	dk green Fr. Knot

Note: Personalize design with DMC 3325 using alphabet on pg. 19.

Design was stitched on a Charles Craft White "Baby Soft" Infant Bib (Item #BB-3650-6750) with a 14 count insert (design size 4³/₄" x 3¹/₂"). Three strands of floss were used for Cross Stitch and 1 strand for Backstitch and French Knots.

Stitch Count (65w x 49h)

14 count	4³/₄"	x	3¹/₂"
16 count	4¹/₈"	x	3¹/₈"
18 count	3⁵/₈"	x	2³/₄"

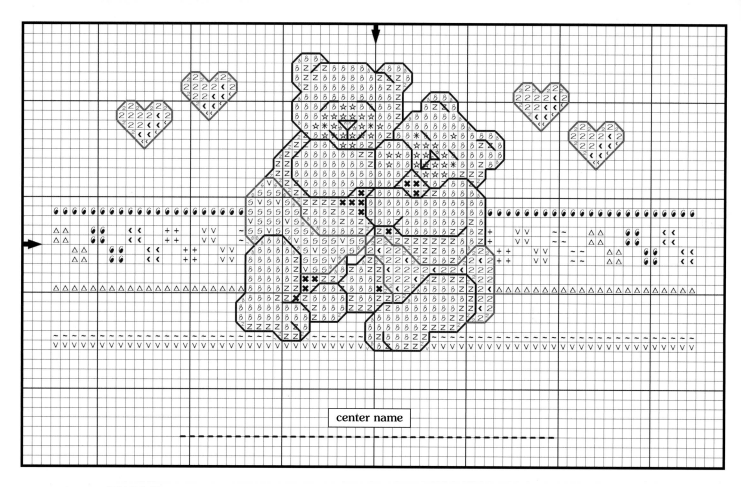

center name

HUG ME

X	DMC	1/4X	B'ST	ANC.	COLOR
☆	blanc	☆		2	white
	150		∕*		dk pink
2	151	2			lt pink
+	210			108	purple
	312		∕*	979	dk blue
	352	n		9	coral
✳	353			6	lt coral
	433		∕	358	dk tan
✖	436			1045	tan
△	727			293	yellow
Z	738	z		361	lt tan
8	739	8		387	vy lt tan
S	775	s		128	lt blue
~	954	~		203	green
V	3325	v		129	blue
6	3340			329	melon
⟨	3733	⟨		75	pink

*DMC 150 for pink diaper and hearts. DMC 312 for blue diaper.

Note: Personalize design with DMC 150 using alphabet on pg. 19.

Design was stitched on a Charles Craft White "Baby Soft" Infant Bib (Item #BB-3650-6750) with a 14 count insert (design size 5" x 2⁷/₈"). Three strands of floss were used for Cross Stitch and 1 strand for Backstitch.

Stitch Count (70w x 40h)

14 count	5"	x	2⁷/₈"
16 count	4³/₈"	x	2¹/₂"
18 count	4"	x	2¹/₄"

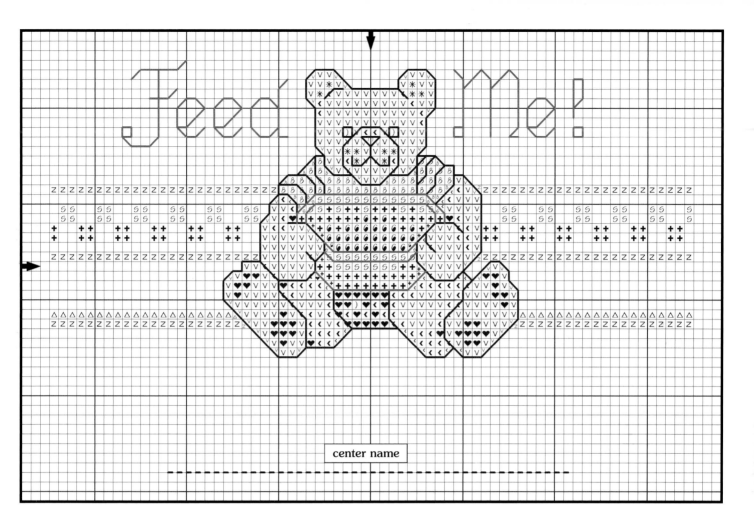

center name

FEED ME!

X DMC	1/4X	B'ST	ANC.	COLOR
312		/*	979	dk blue
* 353			6	coral
) 433	/	/	358	dk tan
♥ 436	/•		1045	tan
8 727	/8		293	yellow
< 738	/<		361	lt tan
V 739	/		387	vy lt tan
△ 775	/△		128	lt blue
910		/*	229	dk green
● 912	/•		209	green
+ 954	/+		203	lt green
5 955	/5		206	vy lt green
Z 3325	/z		129	blue

*DMC 312 for wording. DMC 910 for bowl.

Note: Personalize design with DMC 955 and DMC 3325 using alphabets on pg. 19.

Design was stitched on a Charles Craft White "Baby Soft" Infant Bib (Item #BB-3650-6750) with a 14 count insert (design size 5" x 3¹/₈"). Three strands of floss were used for Cross Stitch and 1 strand for Backstitch.

Stitch Count (70w x 43h)

14 count	5"	x 3¹/₈"
16 count	4³/₈"	x 2³/₄"
18 count	4"	x 2¹/₂"

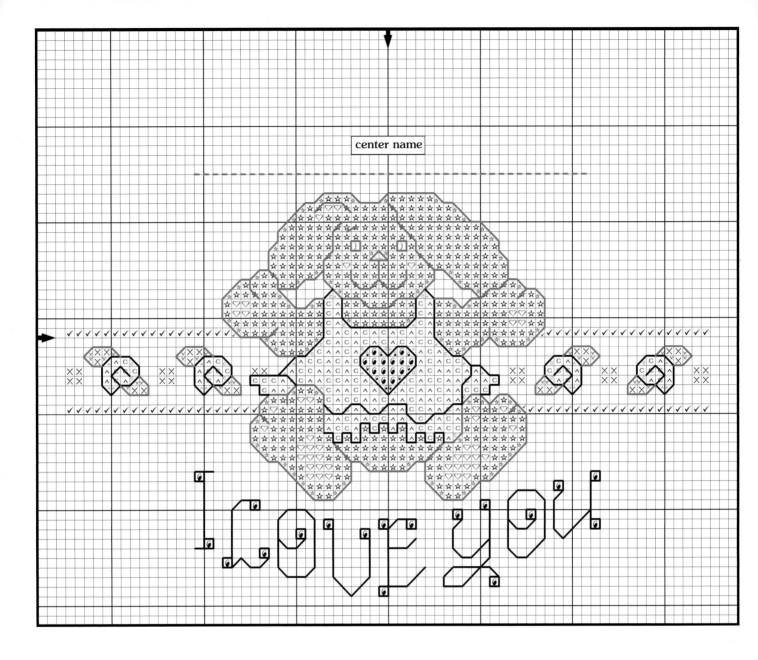

I LOVE YOU

X	DMC	1/4X	B'ST	ANC.	COLOR
☆	blanc	⁄		2	white
◖	150	⁄	⁄		dk pink
∧	151	⁄			lt pink
	352	⁄		9	coral
)	433		⁄*	358	tan
♡	754			1012	peach
✓	775	⁄		128	blue
	910		⁄*	229	green
✕	955	⁄		206	lt green
C	3733	⁄		75	pink

*DMC 433 for bunny. DMC 910 for leaves.

Note: Personalize design with DMC 151 using alphabets on pg. 19.

Design was stitched on a Charles Craft White "Baby Soft" Infant Bib (Item #BB-3650-6750) with a 14 count insert (design size 5" x 3⁷/₈"). Three strands of floss were used for Cross Stitch and 1 strand for Backstitch.

Stitch Count (70w x 54h)

14 count	5"	x	3⁷/₈"
16 count	4³/₈"	x	3³/₈"
18 count	4"	x	3"

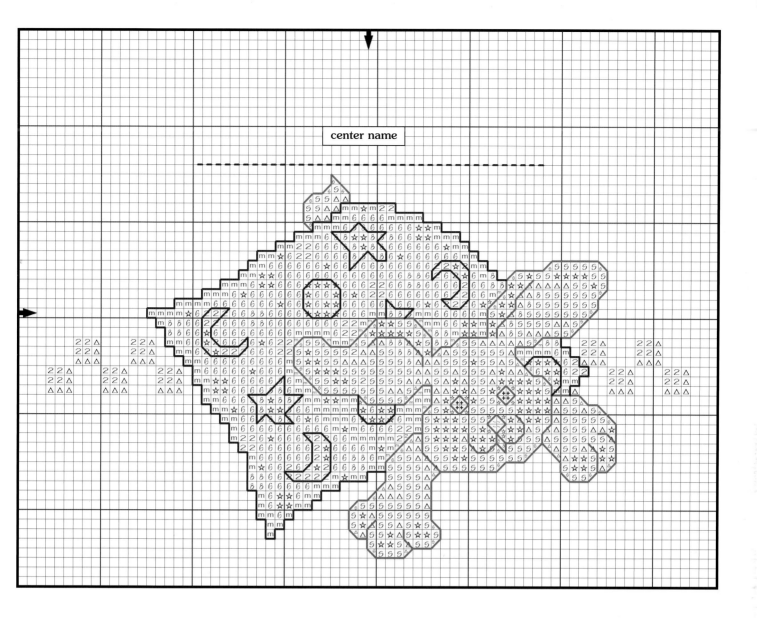

center name

BUNNY AND BLANKET

X	DMC	1/4X	B'ST	ANC.	COLOR
☆	blanc	☆		2	white
	312		/	979	dk blue
	352	-		9	coral
8	754	8		1012	peach
6	775	6		128	lt blue
	910	+	/	229	dk green
△	954	△		203	green
5	955	5		206	lt green
2	3078	2		292	yellow
m	3325	m		129	blue

Design was stitched on a Charles Craft White "Baby Soft" Infant Bib (Item #BB-3650-6750) with a 14 count insert (design size 5" x 3³/₄"). Three strands of floss were used for Cross Stitch and 1 strand for Backstitch.

Stitch Count (70w x 51h)

14 count	5"	x	3³/₄"
16 count	4³/₈"	x	3¹/₄"
18 count	4"	x	2⁷/₈"

Note: Personalize design with DMC 3325 using alphabets on pg. 19.

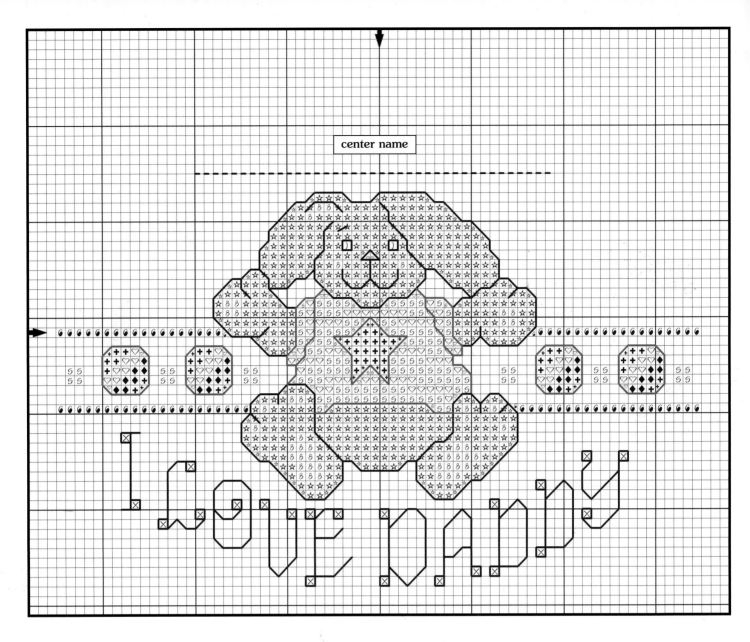

I LOVE DADDY

X	DMC	1/4X	B'ST	ANC.	COLOR
☆	blanc	☆		2	white
✕	312		╱*	979	dk blue
	352	m		9	coral
)	433		╱*	358	tan
+	727	+		293	yellow
8	754			1012	peach
6	775	6		128	lt blue
◆	910		╱	229	green
5	955	5		206	lt green
♡	3755	♡		140	blue

*DMC 312 for wording. DMC 433 for bunny.

Note: Personalize design with DMC 3755 using alphabet on pg. 19.

Design was stitched on a Charles Craft White "Baby Soft" Infant Bib (Item #BB-3650-6750) with a 14 count insert (design size 5" x 3⁷⁄₈"). Three strands of floss were used for Cross Stitch and 1 strand for Backstitch. Bib may be stitched using options on the facing page.

Stitch Count (70w x 53h)

14 count	5"	x	3⁷⁄₈"
16 count	4³⁄₈"	x	3³⁄₈"
18 count	4"	x	3"

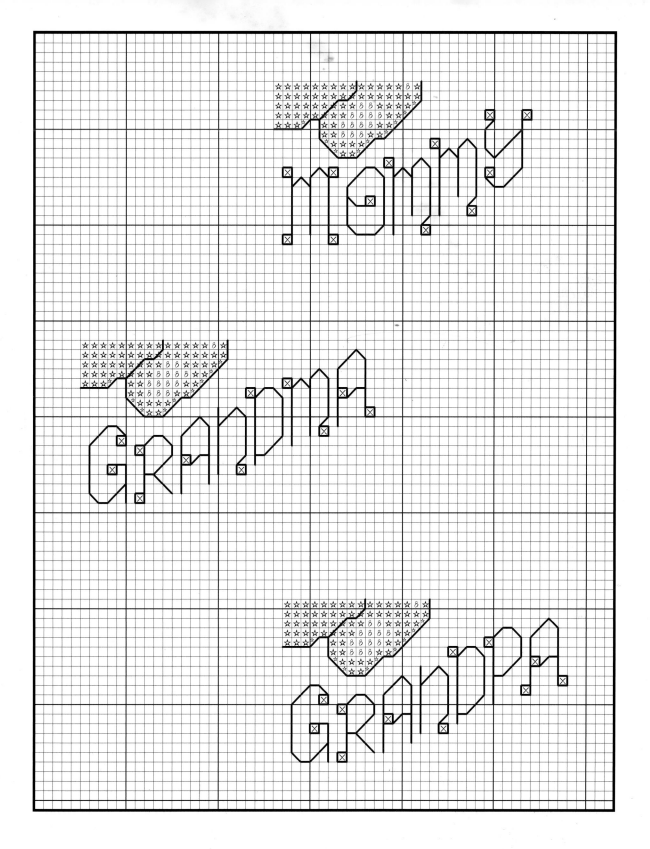

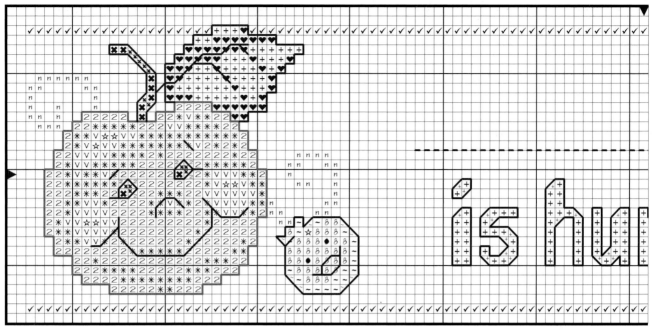

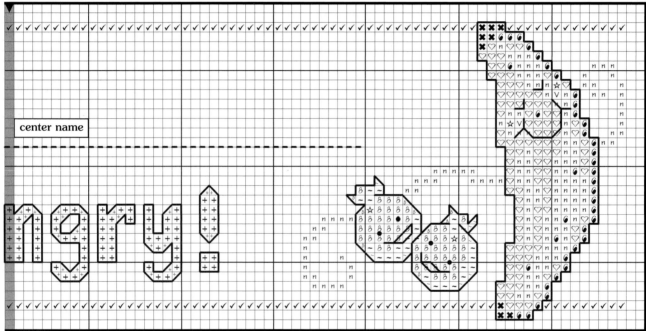

HUNGRY

X	DMC	1/4X	B'ST	ANC.	COLOR
☆	blanc			2	white
	312		∕*	979	blue
2	350	∕2		11	dk coral
✳	351			10	coral
V	352			9	lt coral
♡	726			295	yellow
✓	742			303	dk yellow
8	794	∕8		175	lt royal blue
	816		∕	1005	garnet
✖	838	∕x	∕*	1088	brown
	910		∕*	229	dk green
♥	954			203	green
+	955	∕+		206	lt green

X	DMC	1/4X	ANC.	COLOR
n	3078		292	lt yellow
~	3807	∕-	122	royal blue
6	3852		306	dk gold
●	312		979	blue Fr. Knot
▦	Grey area indicates last row of			
	previous section of design.			

*DMC 312 for blueberries. DMC 838
for apple stem and face and banana.
DMC 910 for leaf and wording.

Note: Personalize design with DMC
352, DMC 726, DMC 794, and
DMC 954 using alphabet on pg. 19.

Design was stitched on a Toddler
Bib with a 14 count insert
(design size 9½" x 2¼").
Three strands of floss were used
for Cross Stitch and 1 strand for
Backstitch and French Knots.

Stitch Count (133w x 31h)
14 count   9½"   x   2¼"
16 count   8⅜"   x   2"
18 count   7½"   x   1¾"

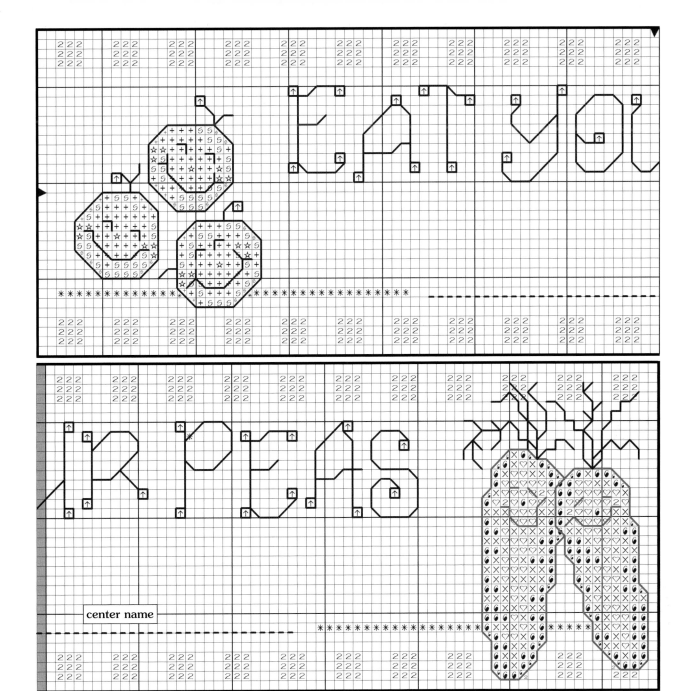

EAT YOUR PEAS

X	DMC	1/4X	B'ST	ANC.	COLOR
☆	blanc			2	white
2	727	◩		293	lt yellow
✕	740			316	lt orange
♡	742			303	yellow
✳	775	◩		128	lt blue
↑	910		◪	229	dk green
●	947	◩		330	orange
5	954	◩		203	green
+	955	◩		206	lt green
	838		◪	1088	brown
	3325			129	blue

▨ Grey area indicates last row of previous section of design.

Note: Personalize design with DMC 3325 using alphabet on pg. 19.

Design was stitched on a Toddler Bib with a 14 count insert (design size $9^3/_8$" x $2^3/_8$"). Three strands of floss were used for Cross Stitch and 1 strand for Backstitch.

Stitch Count (130w x 32h)

14 count	$9^3/_8$"	x $2^3/_8$"
16 count	$8^1/_8$"	x 2"
18 count	$7^1/_4$"	x $1^7/_8$"

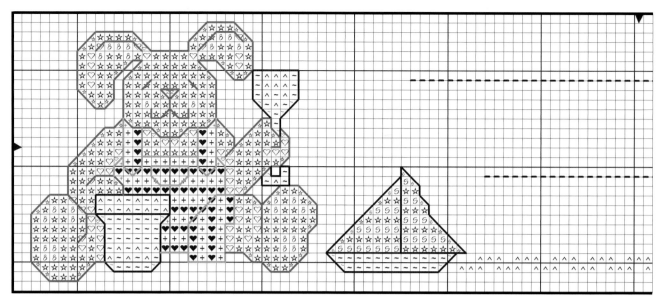

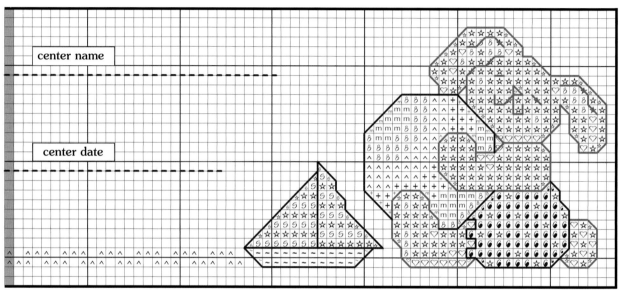

center name

center date

BEACH BUNNIES

X	DMC	1/4X	B'ST	ANC.	COLOR
☆	blanc	☆		2	white
	150		∕*		pink
	312		∕*	979	dk blue
~	334	∕		977	blue
5	350	5		11	coral
	352	2		9	lt coral
8	754	8		1012	peach
	838		∕	1088	brown
♡	842	♡		1080	beige brown
	910		∕	229	dk green
♥	954			203	green
+	955	+		206	lt green
m	3078	m		292	yellow
△	3325	△		129	lt blue

X	DMC	1/4X	ANC.	COLOR
6	3354	6	74	lt pink

Grey area indicates last row of previous section of design.

*DMC 150 for ball and pink outfit.
 DMC 312 for pail, shovel, and sailboats.

Note: Personalize design with DMC 150 using alphabets and numbers on pg. 19.

Design was stitched on a Toddler Bib with a 14 count insert (design size 9³/₈" x 2"). Three strands of floss were used for Cross Stitch and 1 strand for Backstitch.

Stitch Count (131w x 28h)
14 count   9³/₈" x 2"
16 count   8¹/₄" x 1³/₄"
18 count   7³/₈" x 1⁵/₈"

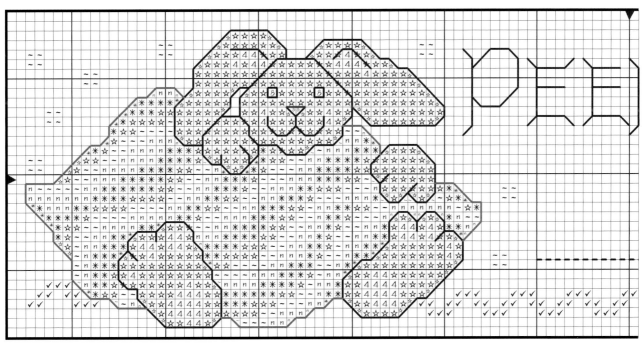

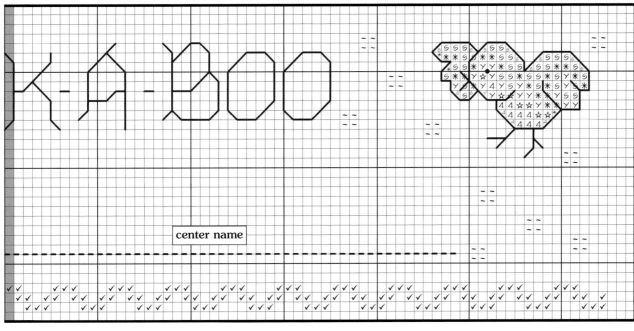

center name

PEEK-A-BOO

X	DMC	¼X	B'ST	ANC.	COLOR
☆	blanc	⊿☆		2	white
	150		⟋*		pink
n	151	⟋n			lt pink
	312		⟋*	979	dk blue
	334		⟋	977	blue
4	754	⊿4		1012	peach
Y	775	⊿Y		128	lt blue
S	793	⊿S		176	royal blue
8	838	⊿8	⟋*	1088	brown
✓	955			206	green
~	3078	⊿-		292	yellow
✳	3325	⊿✳		129	blue

X	DMC	ANC.	COLOR
●	312	979	dk blue Fr. Knot
▨	Grey area indicates last row of previous section of design.		

*DMC 150 for wording. DMC 312 for bird.
DMC 838 for bunny.

Note: Personalize design with DMC 151 using alphabet on pg. 19.

Design was stitched on a Toddler Bib with a 14 count insert (design size 9³⁄₈" x 2¹⁄₄"). Three strands of floss were used for Cross Stitch and 1 strand for Backstitch and French Knot.

Stitch Count (130w x 31h)

14 count	9³⁄₈" x 2¹⁄₄"
16 count	8¹⁄₈" x 2"
18 count	7¹⁄₄" x 1³⁄₄"

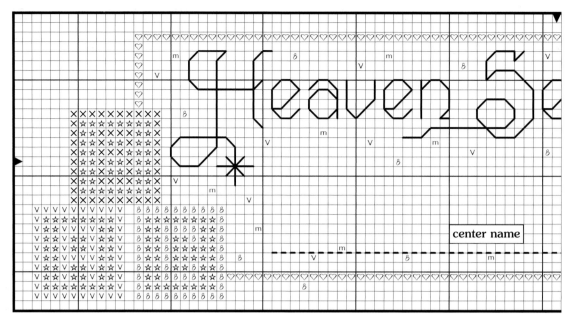

center name

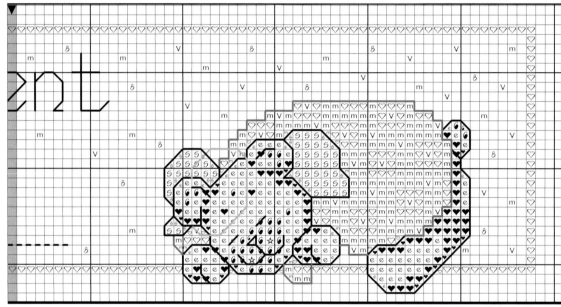

HEAVEN SENT

X	DMC	1/4X	B'ST	ANC.	COLOR
☆	blanc			2	white
	312		╱*	979	dk blue
	433	╱	╱*	358	dk tan
♥	436	╱		1045	tan
◖	712	╱		926	cream
✕	727			293	yellow
e	738	╱		361	lt tan
⑀	775	╱		128	lt blue
	910		╱	229	green
♡	955	╱		206	lt green
m	3078	╱		292	lt yellow
∨	3325			129	blue

X	DMC	B'ST	ANC.	COLOR
⑧	3354		74	lt pink
		╱		Kreinik Metallic #8 Fine Braid #002 gold
▨				Grey area indicates last row of previous section of design.

*DMC 312 for wording, star, and wings.
DMC 433 for bear.

Note: Personalize design with DMC 3325 using alphabets on pg. 19.

Design was stitched on a Toddler Bib with a 14 count insert (design size 8 1/8" x 2"). Three strands of floss were used for Cross Stitch and 1 strand for Backstitch.

Stitch Count (113w x 28h)
14 count	8 1/8"	x 2"
16 count	7 1/8"	x 1 3/4"
18 count	6 3/8"	x 1 5/8"

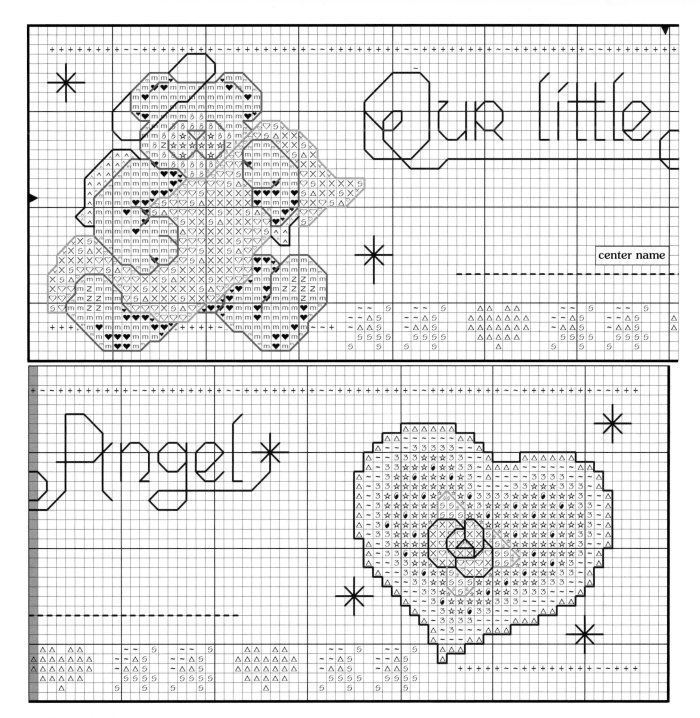

OUR LITTLE ANGEL

X	DMC	1/4X	B'ST	ANC.	COLOR
☆	blanc			2	white
⑥	150		╱*		dk pink
~	151	╱			vy lt pink
③	209			109	purple
	312		╱	979	blue
	433	╱	╱	358	dk tan
♥	436	╱		1045	tan
⑧	712	╱		926	cream
♡	727	╱		293	yellow
m	738	╱		361	lt tan
Z	754			1012	peach
△	775	╱		128	lt blue
	910		╱	229	dk green

X	DMC	1/4X	B'ST	ANC.	COLOR
⑤	954	╱		203	green
+	955	╱		206	lt green
✕	3078	╱		292	lt yellow
△	3731			76	pink
			╱*		Kreinik Metallic
					#8 Fine Braid
					#002 gold

▨ Grey area indicates last row of previous section of design.

*DMC 150 for wording, stars, heart, and flower. DMC 312 for wings. Kreinik Metallic #002 for halo.

Note: Personalize design with DMC 151 using alphabets on pg. 19.

Design was stitched on a Toddler Bib with a 14 count insert (design size 9½" x 2⅜"). Three strands of floss were used for Cross Stitch and 1 strand for Backstitch.

Stitch Count (133w x 32h)
14 count	9½"	x	2⅜"
16 count	8⅜"	x	2"
18 count	7½"	x	1⅞"

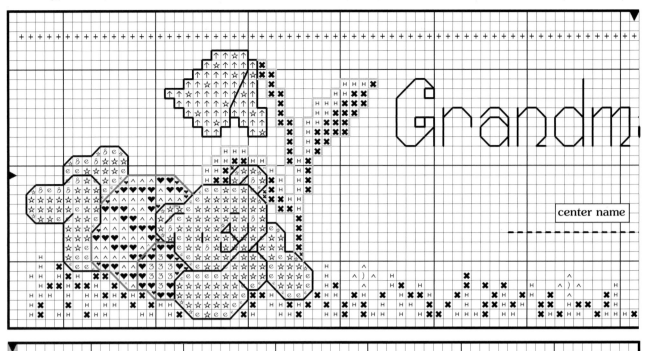

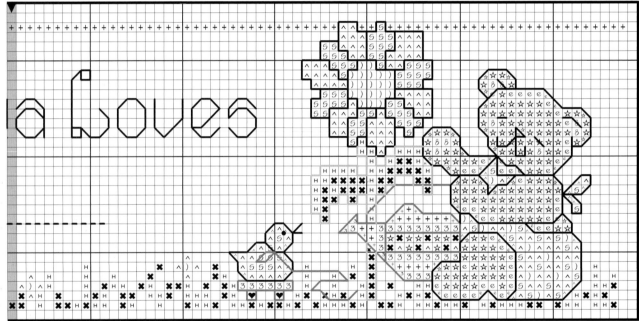

BEAR FRIENDS

X	DMC	1/4X	B'ST	ANC.	COLOR
☆	blanc	✓		2	white
	150		✓*		pink
↑	151				lt pink
	312		✓	979	dk blue
♥	334	✓		977	blue
	352	✓m		9	coral
8	353			6	lt coral
∧	726	✓		295	yellow
+	775	✓		128	vy lt blue
)	838		✓*	1088	brown
	910		✓	229	dk green
✖	912	✓		209	green

X	DMC	1/4X	ANC.	COLOR
H	955	✓	206	lt green
3	3325	✓	129	lt blue
5	3820		306	gold
e	3866	✓	926	beige brown
●	838		1088	brown Fr. Knot

Grey area indicates last row of previous section of design.

*DMC 150 for pink flower and wording.
DMC 838 for bears, yellow and brown outfit, duck, and yellow flower.

Note: Personalize design with DMC 150 using alphabets on pg. 19.

Design was stitched on a Toddler Bib with a 14 count insert (design size 9½" x 2¼"). Three strands of floss were used for Cross Stitch and 1 strand for Backstitch and French Knot.

Stitch Count (133w x 30h)

14 count	9½"	x 2¼"
16 count	8³⁄₈"	x 1⁷⁄₈"
18 count	7½"	x 1³⁄₄"

HOW TO READ CHARTS

Each chart is made up of a key and a gridded design where each square represents a stitch. The symbols in the key tell which floss color to use for each stitch in the chart. The following headings and symbols are given:

X — Cross Stitch
DMC — DMC color number
¼X — Quarter Stitch
B'ST — Backstitch
ANC. — Anchor color number
COLOR — the name given to the floss color in this chart

A square with a symbol should be worked as a **Cross Stitch**.

A a reduced symbol should be worked as a **Quarter Stitch**.

A straight line should be worked as a **Backstitch**.

A large dot listed near the end of the key should be worked as a **French Knot**.

HOW TO STITCH

Always work **Cross Stitches** and **Quarter Stitches** first and then add the **Backstitch** and **French Knots**.

Cross Stitch (X): For horizontal rows, work stitches in two journeys *(Fig. 1)*. For vertical rows, complete each stitch as shown *(Fig. 2)*.

Fig. 1

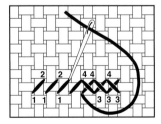

Fig. 2

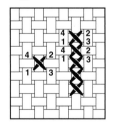

Quarter Stitch (¼X): Come up at 1, then split fabric thread to go down at 2 *(Fig. 3)*.

Fig. 3

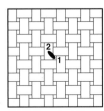

Backstitch (B'ST): For outlines and details, Backstitch should be worked after the design has been completed *(Fig. 4)*.

Fig. 4

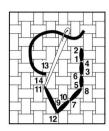

French Knot: Bring needle up at 1. Wrap floss once around needle. Insert needle at 2, tighten knot, and pull needle through fabric, holding floss until it must be released *(Fig. 5)*. For a larger knot, use more floss strands; wrap only once.

Fig. 5

STITCHING TIPS

Working with Floss

To ensure smoother stitches, separate strands and realign them before threading needle. Keep stitching tension consistent. Begin and end floss by running under several stitches on back; never tie knots.

Where to Start

The horizontal and vertical centers of each charted design are shown by arrows. You may start at any point on the charted design, but be sure the design will be centered on the fabric. Locate the center of fabric by folding in half, top to bottom and again left to right. On the charted design, count the number of squares (stitches) from the center of the chart to where you wish to start. Then from the fabric's center, find your starting point by counting out the same number of fabric threads (stitches).